尼克·胡哲

Heroes and Role Models | Non-Fiction Series

Copyright © 2022 by Level Learning, INC. and Washington Yu Ying PCS™
Original and Edited Text Copyright © 2022 by Washington Yu Ying PCS™

All rights reserved. No part of this book in whole or part may be reproduced without written permission from the publisher.

Published by Level Learning, INC.

Content Contributors:
Washington Yu Ying PCS™
Level Learning - Ya-Ching Chang

Illustrations by: Josh Taira

Leveling classification based on Level Learning standard. For full description, visit www.levellearning.com

ISBN 978-1-64040-006-1
Simplified Chinese Edition

About Level Learning:
Level Learning provides a literacy focused curriculum specifically designed for K-12 Chinese as a Second Language classrooms. Our program offers 20 levels of specific and detailed objectives, leveled texts and passages, mastery-based online assessment, and analytics to enable data-driven instruction. Level Learning reading curriculum for both literature and informational text emphasize grammar and comprehension skills to help teachers develop confident and independent Chinese language readers. The non-fiction series of books are specifically designed to support our informational text course based on multiple national standards. To learn more about our entire offering, visit www.levellearning.com

About Washington Yu Ying PCS™:
Washington Yu Ying PCS is a Mandarin English dual language immersion International Baccalaureate (IB) World school. Yu Ying's mission is to inspire and prepare young people to create a better world by challenging them to reach their full potential in a nurturing Chinese/English educational environment. Yu Ying's comprehensive IB, dual immersion curriculum equips students with global competencies for success in the real world. As a leader in immersion education, Yu Ying is determined to advance Chinese language programs and global citizenry education by helping other schools create and strengthen their Chinese programs. For more information, email: products@washingtonyuying.org

有一个人,他的名字叫尼克。他出生的时候,没有手,没有脚。

但是，尼克有爱他的家人。尼克也有对生活的希望。

没有手，尼克可以用嘴巴写字。

没有脚,尼克可以用身体运动。

没有手和脚,尼克也可以去大学读书。

没有手和脚,尼克也可以去很多国家旅行。

没有手和脚,尼克也可以去不同的地方演讲。

感恩的心

尼克可以做很多事情。我们看到了尼克对生活的希望。

Glossary

	Pinyin	English Definition
出生	chū shēng	born
爱	ài	love
生活	shēng huó	life
希望	xī wàng	hope
写字	xiě zì	to write
运动	yùn dòng	to exercise
国家	guó jiā	country
旅行	lǚ xíng	to travel
演讲	yǎn jiǎng	to give speeches

www.ingramcontent.com/pod-product-compliance
Lightning Source LLC
Chambersburg PA
CBHW041224070526
44584CB00001B/87